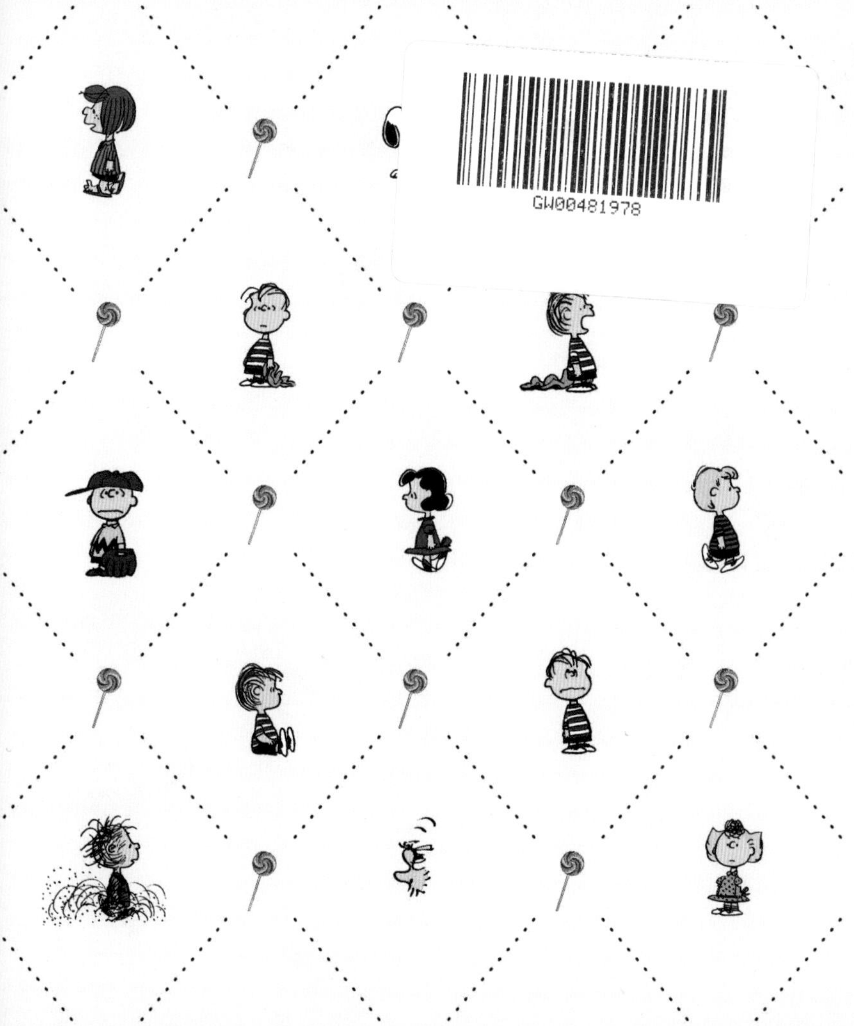

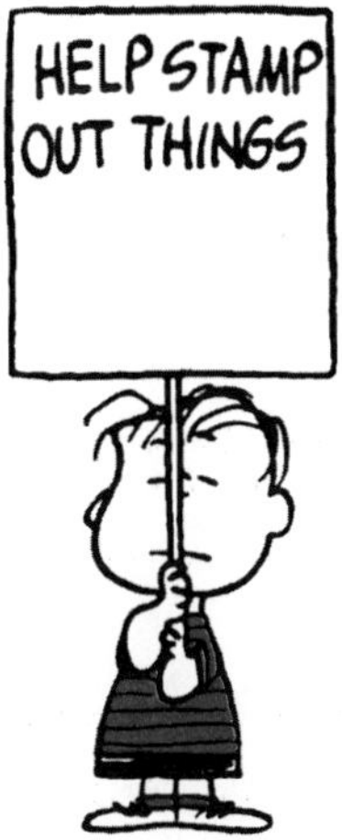
HELP STAMP
OUT THINGS

Published in Great Britain in 2016 by Canongate Books Ltd,
14 High Street, Edinburgh EH1 1TE

www.canongate.tv

1

British Library Cataloguing-in-Publication Data
A catalogue record for this book is available on
request from the British Library

ISBN 978 1 78211 371 3

PEANUTS written and drawn by Charles M. Schulz
Edited by Jenny Lord and Andy Miller
Design: Rafaela Romaya
Layout: Stuart Polson

Printed in China by C&C Offset Printing Co, Ltd

CHARLES M. SCHULZ

LIFE ACCORDING TO
LINUS

CANONGATE

Edinburgh · London

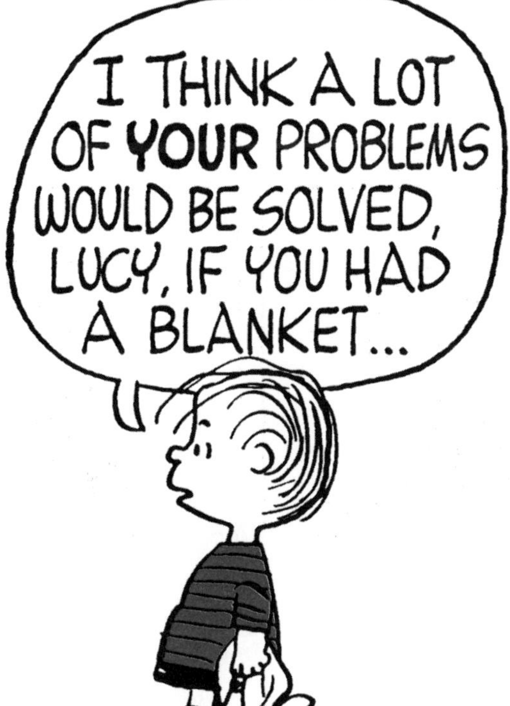
I THINK A LOT OF **YOUR** PROBLEMS WOULD BE SOLVED, LUCY, IF YOU HAD A BLANKET...

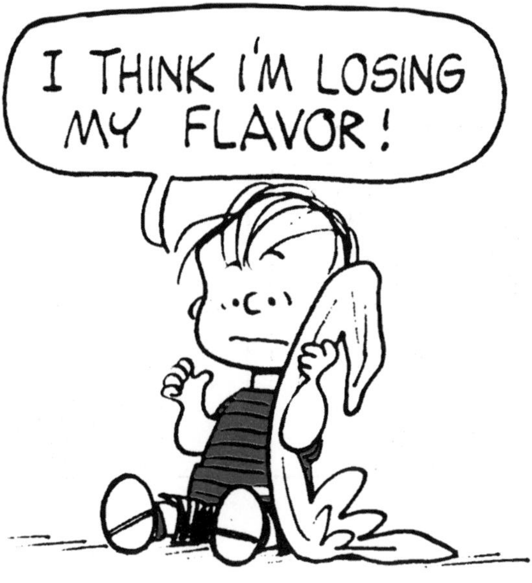
I THINK I'M LOSING MY FLAVOR!

IF I WERE YOU, I'D BE AFRAID OF WHAT THE KIDS IN SCHOOL WOULD SAY ABOUT THAT BLANKET..
DO YOU HAVE A NICKEL? TOSS IT IN THE AIR...

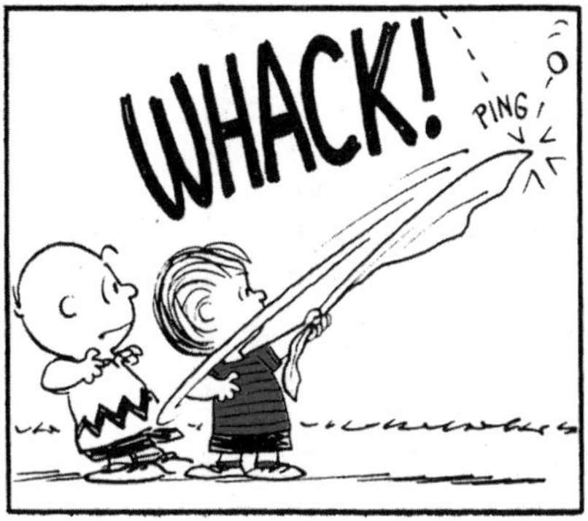
WHACK!
PING

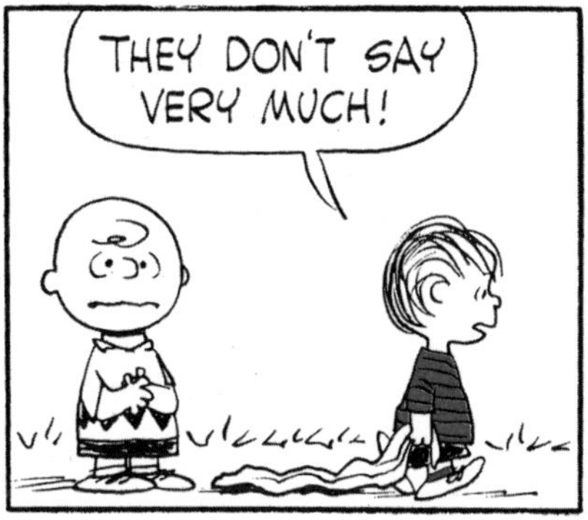
THEY DON'T SAY VERY MUCH!

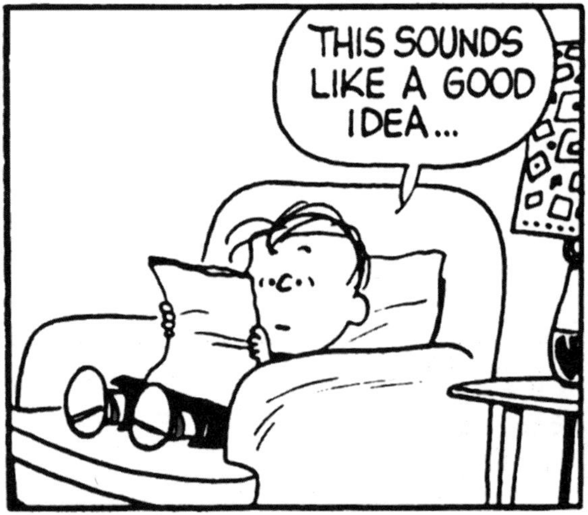
THIS SOUNDS LIKE A GOOD IDEA...

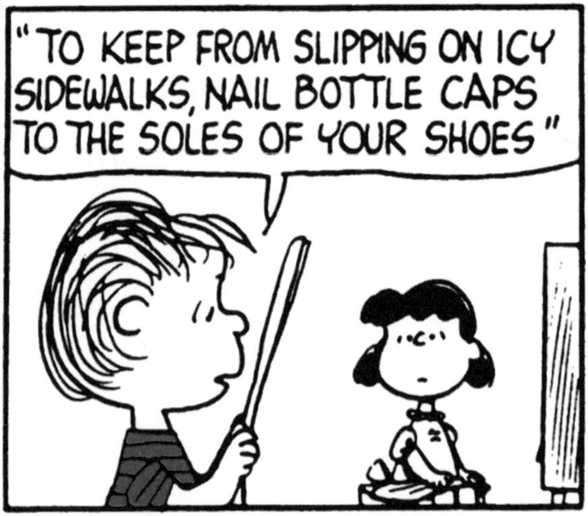
"TO KEEP FROM SLIPPING ON ICY SIDEWALKS, NAIL BOTTLE CAPS TO THE SOLES OF YOUR SHOES"

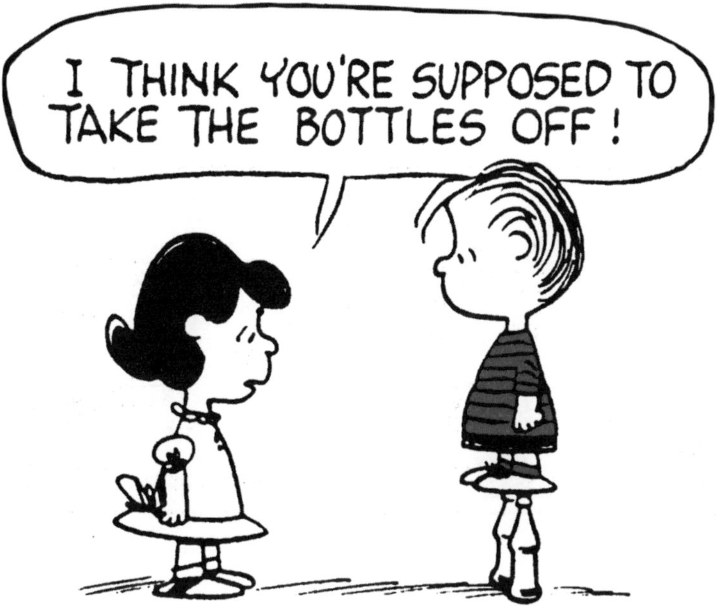
I THINK YOU'RE SUPPOSED TO TAKE THE BOTTLES OFF !

PAT
PAT
PAT
PAT

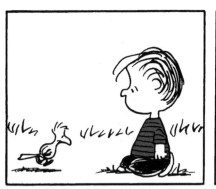

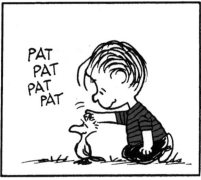

THEY COME DEPRESSED, AND THEY GO AWAY FEELING GREAT

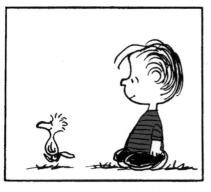

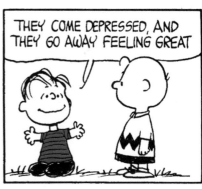

ALL RIGHT, WHERE IS IT?!
SOMEBODY HAS MY BLANKET, AND WHEN I FIND HIM, I'LL FIX HIM GOOD! I'M MAD! I'M REALLY MAD!!

I'LL FIND HIM, TOO! I'LL FIND WHOEVER TOOK MY BLANKET, AND WHEN I'M THROUGH WITH HIM HE'LL BE PLENTY SORRY!!

CHARLIE BROWN SAYS THAT BROTHERS AND SISTERS CAN LEARN TO GET ALONG...
HE SAYS THEY CAN GET ALONG THE SAME WAY MATURE ADULTS GET ALONG...

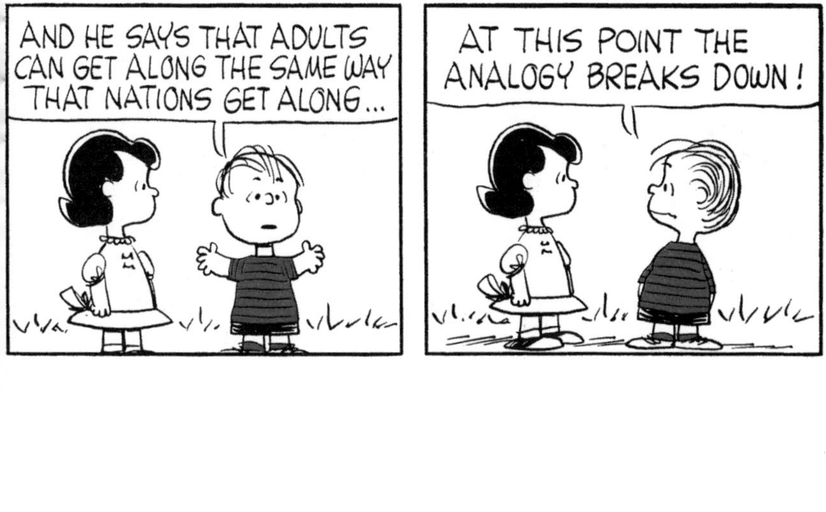
AND HE SAYS THAT ADULTS CAN GET ALONG THE SAME WAY THAT NATIONS GET ALONG...
AT THIS POINT THE ANALOGY BREAKS DOWN!

HERE..MOM JUST TOOK SOME OF YOUR SOCKS OUT OF THE DRYER..
SHE SAID FOR YOU TO PUT THEM IN YOUR DRESSER

SECURITY IS HAVING A
DRAWER-FULL OF WARM SOCKS!

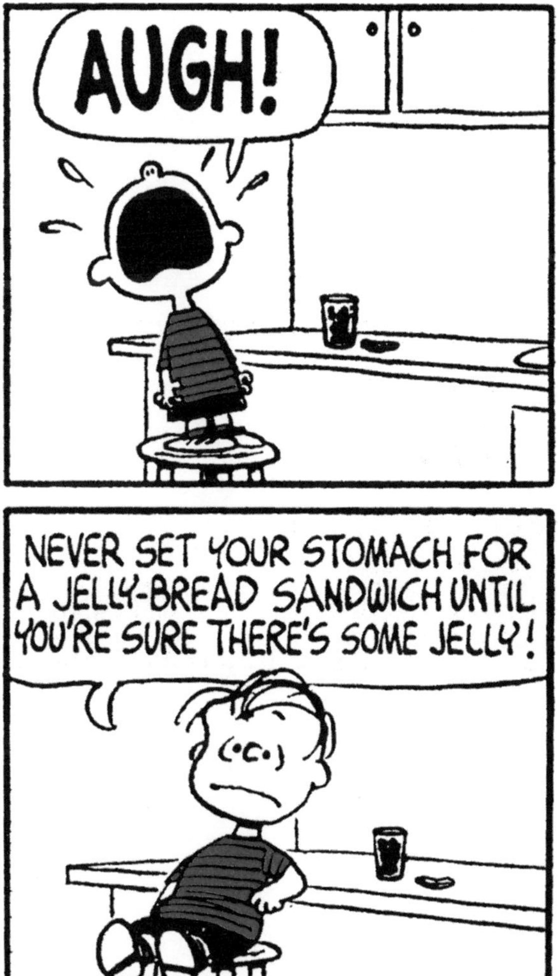
AUGH!
NEVER SET YOUR STOMACH FOR A JELLY-BREAD SANDWICH UNTIL YOU'RE SURE THERE'S SOME JELLY!

HEY! GET UP! AREN'T YOU GOING TO SCHOOL?
I DON'T THINK SO...

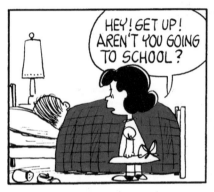

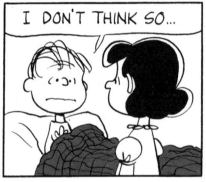

I'VE GOT A PAIN..
TELL MOM I THINK MY STOMACH IS BROKEN!

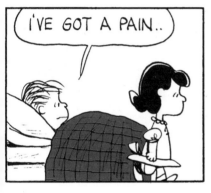

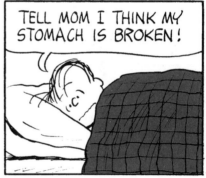

WHAT'S THIS?
A DISH OF ICE CREAM
I BROUGHT IT TO YOU IN ORDER THAT YOUR STAY HERE ON EARTH MIGHT BE MORE PLEASANT

WELL, THANK YOU...YOU'RE A GOOD BROTHER..
HAPPINESS IS A COMPLIMENT FROM YOUR SISTER!

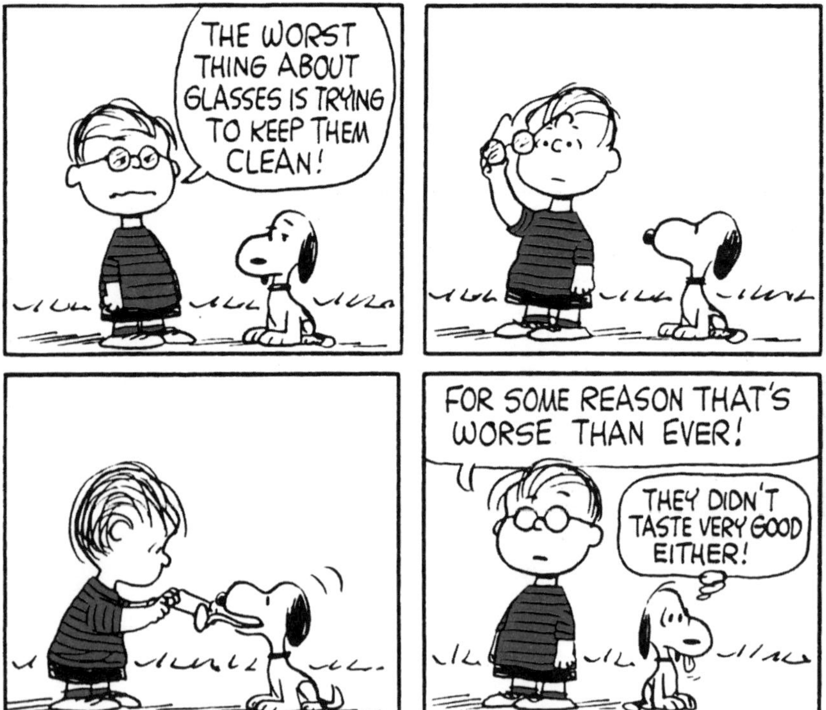
THE WORST THING ABOUT GLASSES IS TRYING TO KEEP THEM CLEAN!
FOR SOME REASON THAT'S WORSE THAN EVER!
THEY DIDN'T TASTE VERY GOOD EITHER!

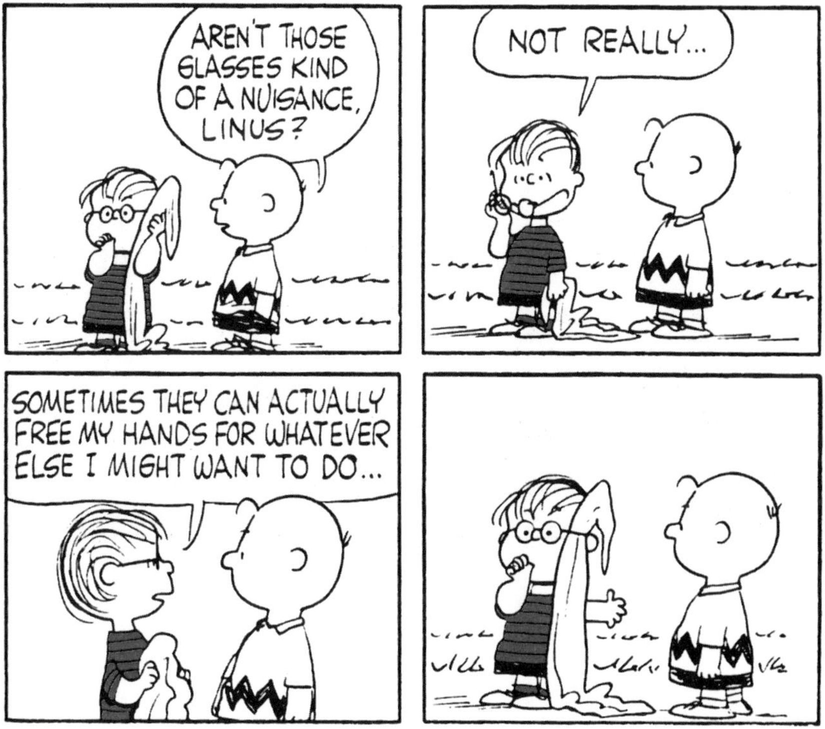
AREN'T THOSE GLASSES KIND OF A NUISANCE, LINUS?
NOT REALLY...
SOMETIMES THEY CAN ACTUALLY FREE MY HANDS FOR WHATEVER ELSE I MIGHT WANT TO DO...

NO, THAT'S TOO LOOSE... I FEEL FLIMSY...
HOW'S THAT?
TOO TIGHT! TOO TIGHT! AAUGH!

ALL RIGHT, HOW'S THAT?
WHEW! THAT'S FINE! YES, THAT'S FINE! WHEW!
I CAN'T EVEN BREATHE IF MY SHOELACES AREN'T TIED JUST RIGHT!

YOU'RE THINKING OF KICKING OVER MY SAND CASTLE, AREN'T YOU?
WELL, WAIT JUST A MOMENT, WILL YOU, PLEASE, WHILE I STAND UP?

THIS WILL GIVE ME A CHANCE TO..
BEAT YOU TO IT!!!

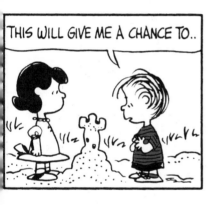

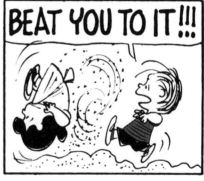

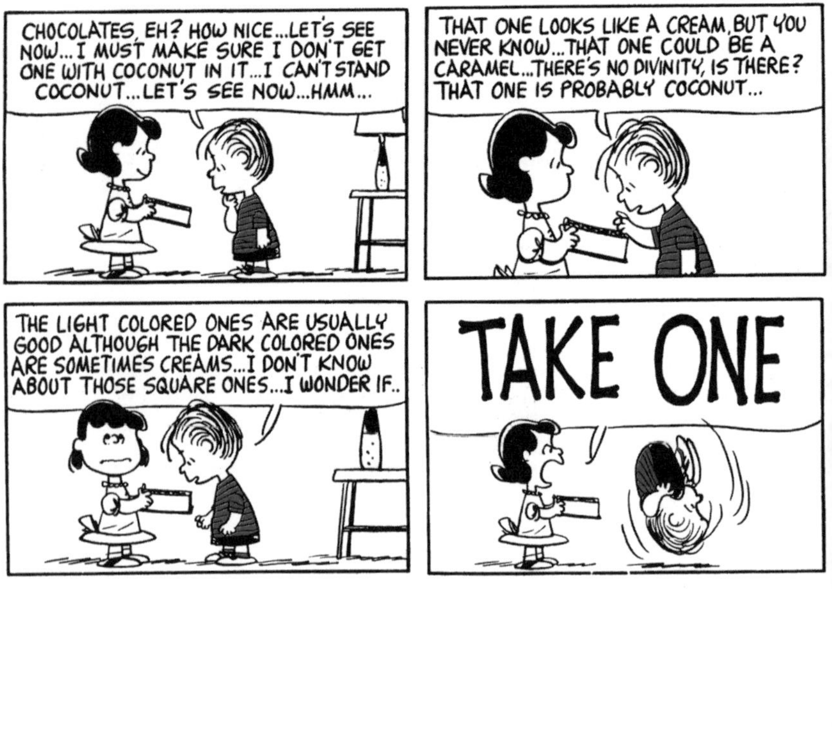
CHOCOLATES, EH? HOW NICE...LET'S SEE NOW...I MUST MAKE SURE I DON'T GET ONE WITH COCONUT IN IT...I CAN'T STAND COCONUT...LET'S SEE NOW...HMM...
THAT ONE LOOKS LIKE A CREAM, BUT YOU NEVER KNOW...THAT ONE COULD BE A CARAMEL...THERE'S NO DIVINITY, IS THERE? THAT ONE IS PROBABLY COCONUT...
THE LIGHT COLORED ONES ARE USUALLY GOOD ALTHOUGH THE DARK COLORED ONES ARE SOMETIMES CREAMS...I DON'T KNOW ABOUT THOSE SQUARE ONES...I WONDER IF..
TAKE ONE

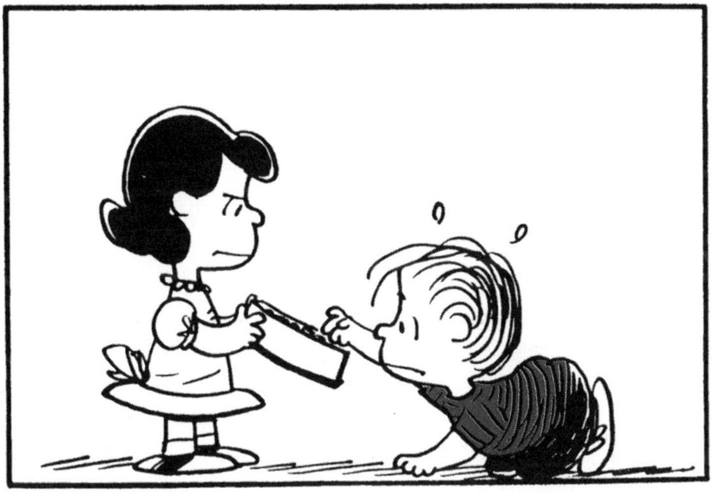

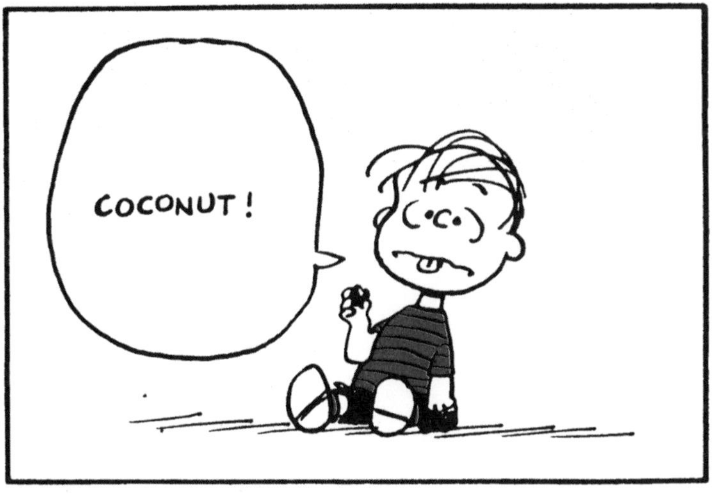
COCONUT!

I CAN'T STAND THAT COMMERCIAL !

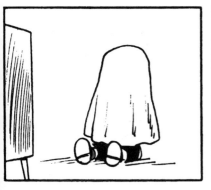

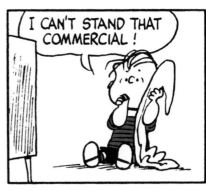

MOM SAYS TO GET YOUR COAT ON.. WE'RE GOING TO GO GET A MEASLES SHOT...
A MEASLES SHOT?

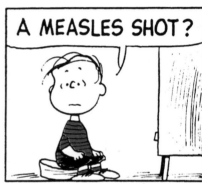

GOOD GRIEF, EVERY TIME I TURN AROUND, I GET SHOT FOR SOMETHING
WHAT DOES THAT PEDIATRICIAN THINK I AM, A DART BOARD?!

PAT PAT PAT PAT PAT
SIGH

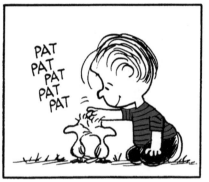

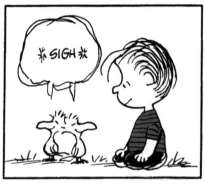

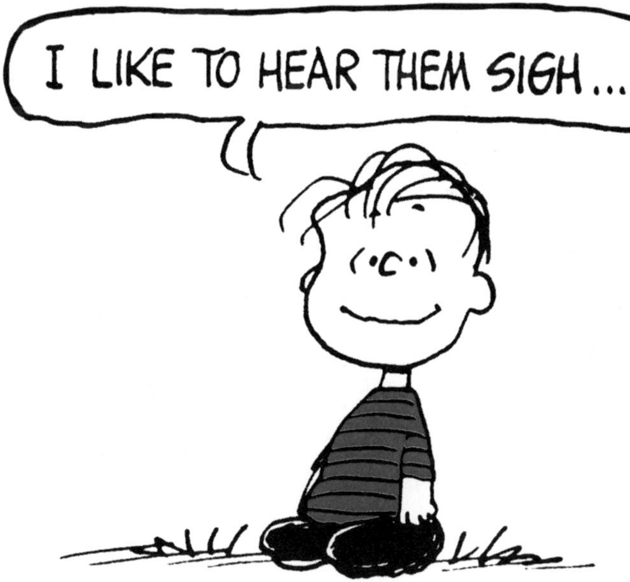
I LIKE TO HEAR THEM SIGH...

SCHOOL IS OVER!
I'VE NEVER BEEN SO HAPPY IN ALL MY LIFE!

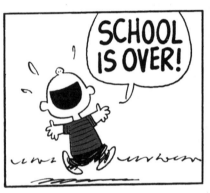

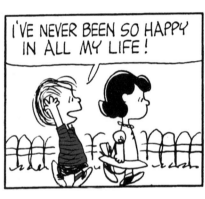

I FEEL LIKE A GREAT BURDEN HAS BEEN LIFTED FROM MY SHOULDERS...
WHAT SHOULDERS?

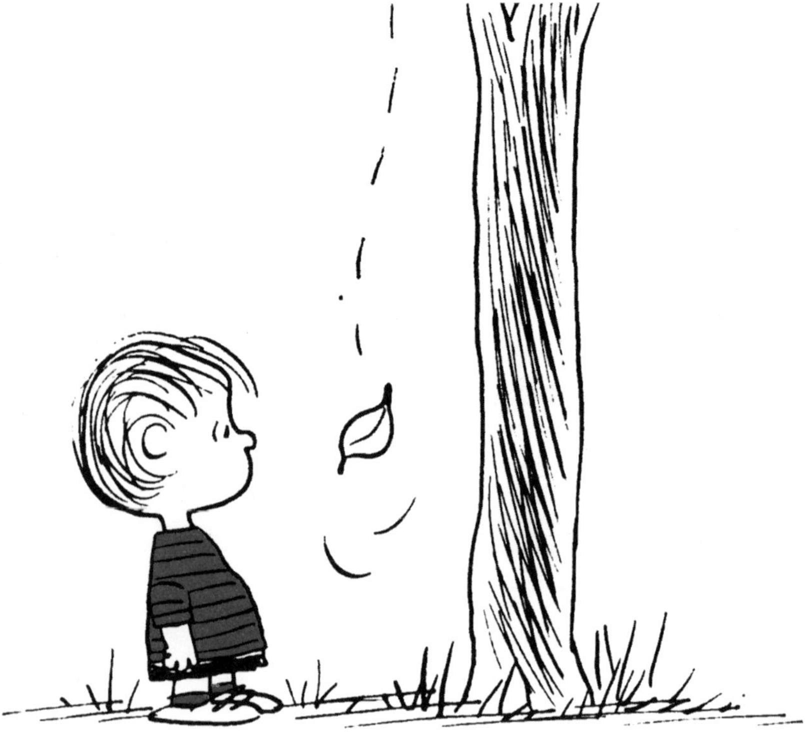

NOW LOOK WHAT YOU'VE DONE... YOU'VE BURIED YOUR LEADER!

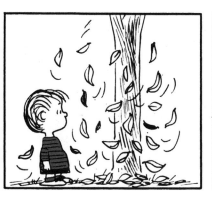

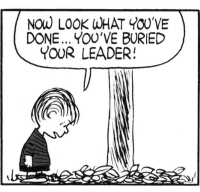

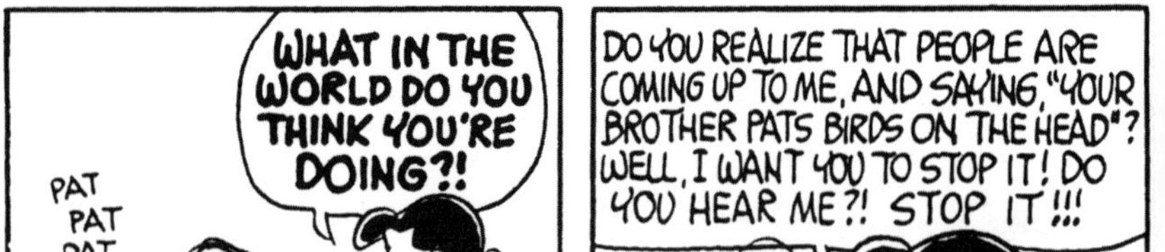

WHAT IN THE WORLD DO YOU THINK YOU'RE DOING?!
PAT PAT PAT PAT
SIGH!
DO YOU REALIZE THAT PEOPLE ARE COMING UP TO ME, AND SAYING, "YOUR BROTHER PATS BIRDS ON THE HEAD"? WELL, I WANT YOU TO STOP IT! DO YOU HEAR ME?! STOP IT!!!

TRIP!

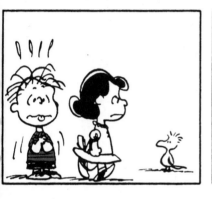

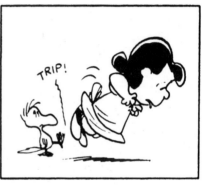

WHAT ARE YOU DOING OUT HERE?
I'M WAITING FOR THE "GREAT PUMPKIN" TO APPEAR
YOU HAVE A LONG WAIT... HALLOWEEN ISN'T UNTIL NEXT TUESDAY..
I DON'T CARE.. IT'S VERY PEACEFUL OUT HERE...
MOST PSYCHIATRISTS AGREE THAT SITTING IN A PUMPKIN PATCH IS EXCELLENT THERAPY FOR A TROUBLED MIND!

HEY, WAKE UP... HALLOWEEN IS OVER..YOU MISSED THE GREAT PUMPKIN!
IT JUST CAME OVER THE RADIO..HE APPEARED IN A VERY SINCERE PUMPKIN PATCH OWNED BY SOMEONE NAMED FREEMAN IN NEW JERSEY!
OH, GREAT PUMPKIN, YOU'RE GOING TO DRIVE ME CRAZY!!!

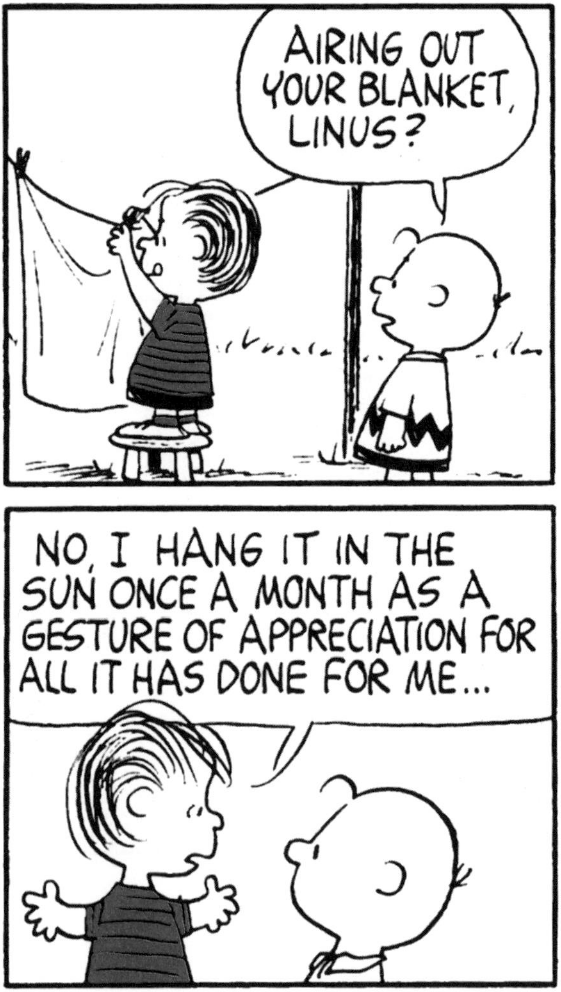
AIRING OUT YOUR BLANKET, LINUS?
NO, I HANG IT IN THE SUN ONCE A MONTH AS A GESTURE OF APPRECIATION FOR ALL IT HAS DONE FOR ME...

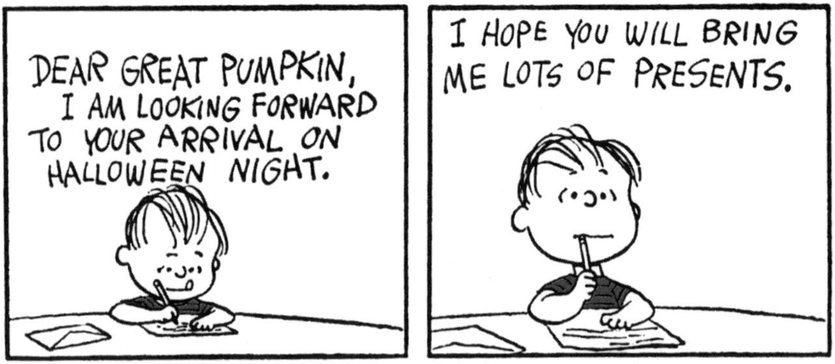
DEAR GREAT PUMPKIN,
I AM LOOKING FORWARD TO YOUR ARRIVAL ON HALLOWEEN NIGHT.
I HOPE YOU WILL BRING ME LOTS OF PRESENTS.

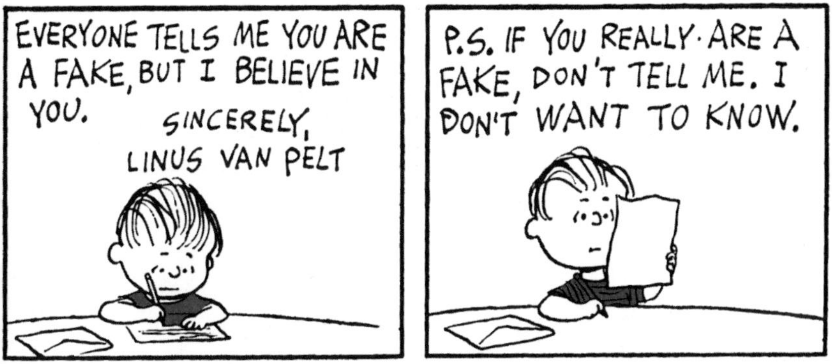
EVERYONE TELLS ME YOU ARE A FAKE, BUT I BELIEVE IN YOU.
SINCERELY, LINUS VAN PELT
P.S. IF YOU REALLY ARE A FAKE, DON'T TELL ME. I DON'T WANT TO KNOW.

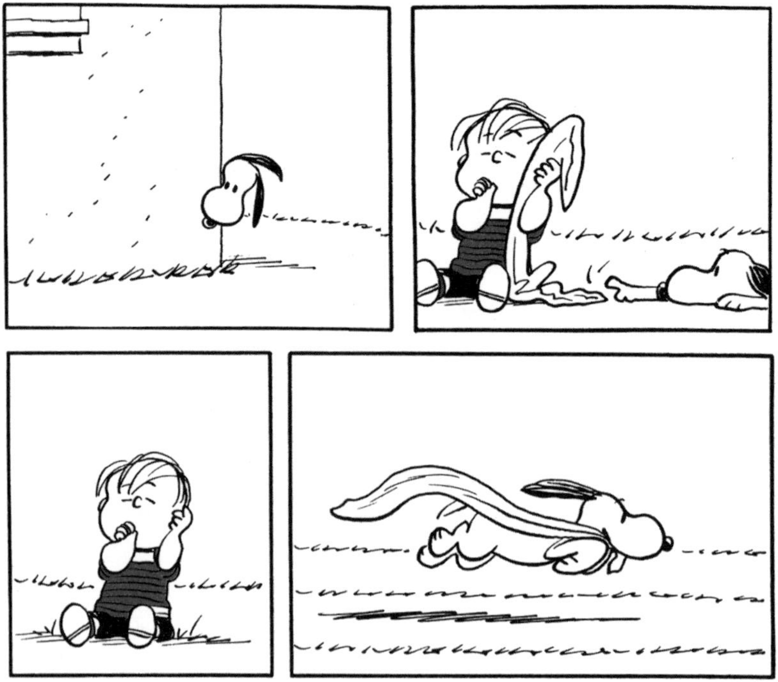

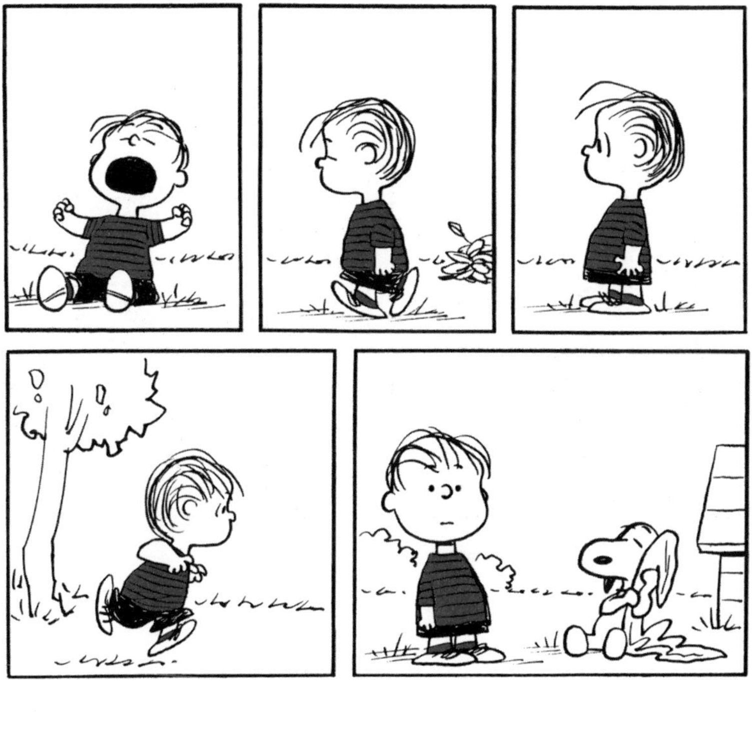

DID YOU FILL OUT THAT PAPER FOR THE SCHOOL OFFICE?
I HAVE IT RIGHT HERE...
MY MOTHER'S NAME, MY FATHER'S NAME, OUR ADDRESS AND OUR TELEPHONE NUMBER...

WHAT DID YOU PUT DOWN UNDER "FAMILY PHYSICIAN"?
WELL, I WASN'T SURE SO I PUT DOWN "DR. SEUSS"!

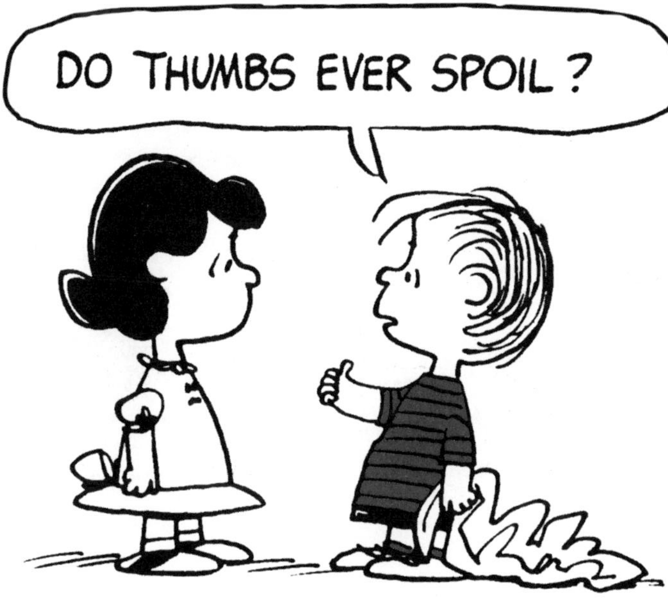
DO THUMBS EVER SPOIL?

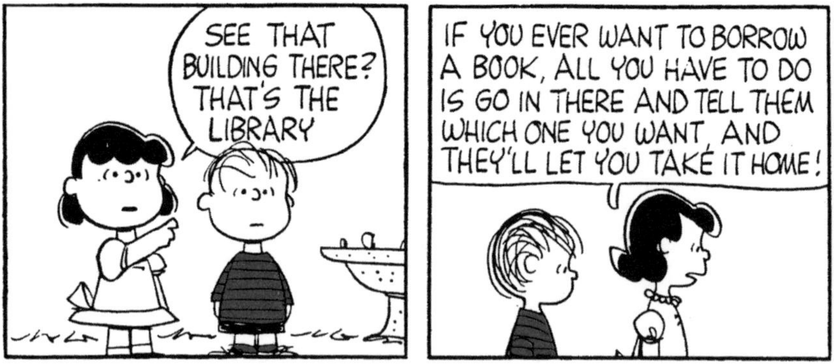
SEE THAT BUILDING THERE? THAT'S THE LIBRARY
IF YOU EVER WANT TO BORROW A BOOK, ALL YOU HAVE TO DO IS GO IN THERE AND TELL THEM WHICH ONE YOU WANT, AND THEY'LL LET YOU TAKE IT HOME!

FREE?
ABSOLUTELY FREE!
SORT OF MAKES YOU WONDER WHAT THEY'RE UP TO!

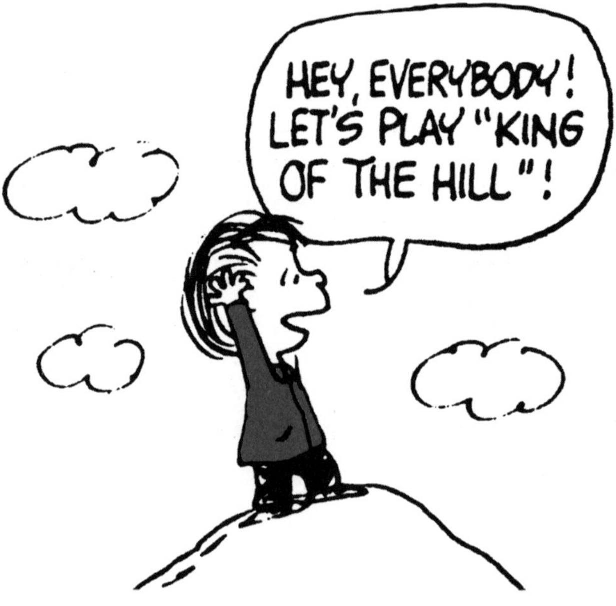
HEY, EVERYBODY! LET'S PLAY "KING OF THE HILL"!

ALL RIGHT, LET'S PLAY "QUEEN OF THE HILL"

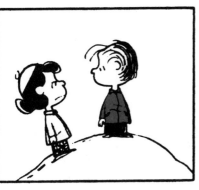

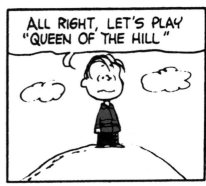

MOM SAYS TO COME AND EMPTY ALL THE WASTE BASKETS
OH, RATS!

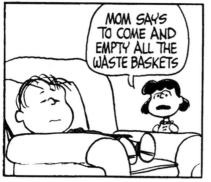

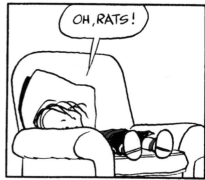

I DON'T LIKE TO DO ANYTHING THAT INTERFERES WITH MY NOT DOING ANYTHING!

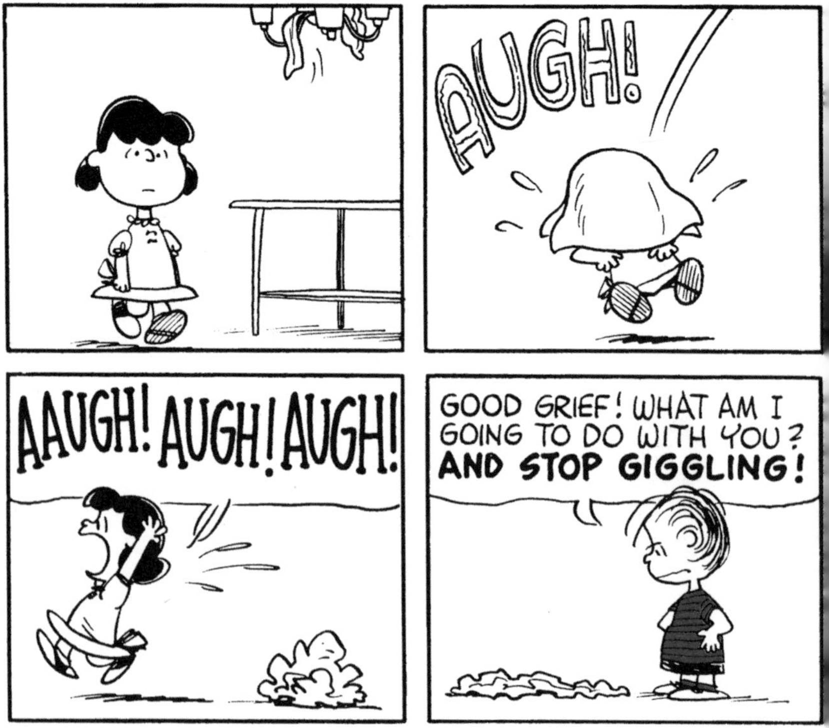
AUGH!
AAUGH! AUGH! AUGH!
GOOD GRIEF! WHAT AM I GOING TO DO WITH YOU? AND STOP GIGGLING!

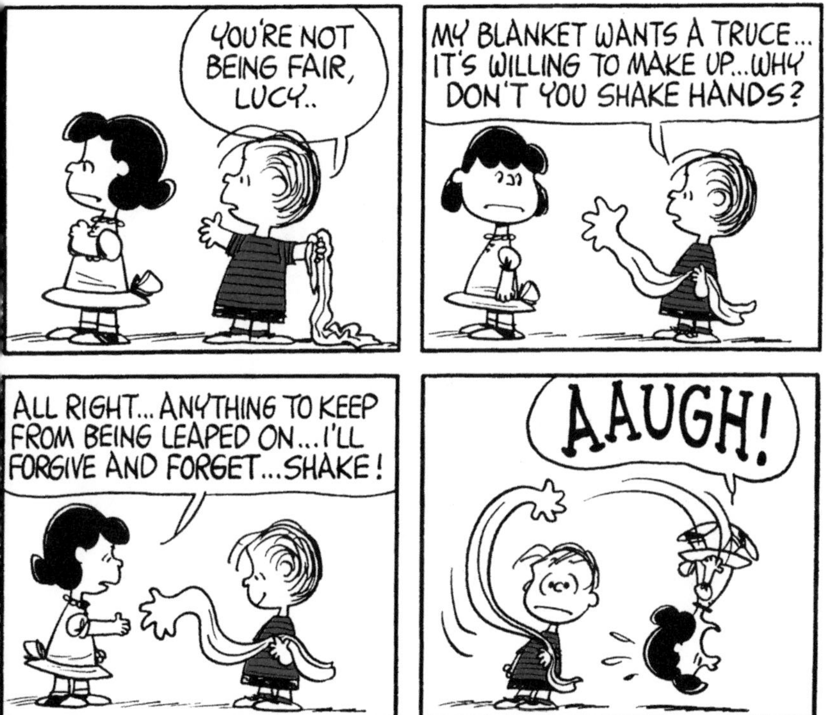
YOU'RE NOT BEING FAIR, LUCY..
MY BLANKET WANTS A TRUCE... IT'S WILLING TO MAKE UP...WHY DON'T YOU SHAKE HANDS?
ALL RIGHT...ANYTHING TO KEEP FROM BEING LEAPED ON...I'LL FORGIVE AND FORGET...SHAKE!
AAUGH!

KER-LEAF!
"KER-LEAF"?!!

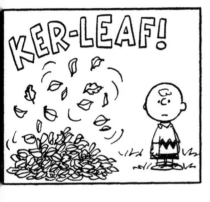

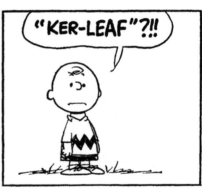

DEAR SANTA CLAUS,
HOW HAVE YOU BEEN?
HOW IS YOUR WIFE?
I AM NOT SURE WHAT I WANT FOR CHRISTMAS THIS YEAR.

SOMETIMES IT IS VERY HARD TO DECIDE.
PERHAPS YOU SHOULD SEND ME YOUR CATALOGUE.

I AM THINKING OF YOOO TONIGHT!
CAN'T YOU EVER BE QUIET?!
YOU'RE THE NOISIEST PERSON WHO EVER LIVED!
IF YOU'RE NOT SINGING, YOU'RE KNOCKING THINGS OVER OR RUNNING THROUGH THE HOUSE LIKE YOU'RE CRAZY!

AND TURN THAT STUPID TV DOWN
SIGH
Bread
WHAT ARE YOU DOING NOW?
MAKING MYSELF A BREAD AND BUTTER SANDWICH..
AM I BUTTERING TOO LOUD FOR YOU?

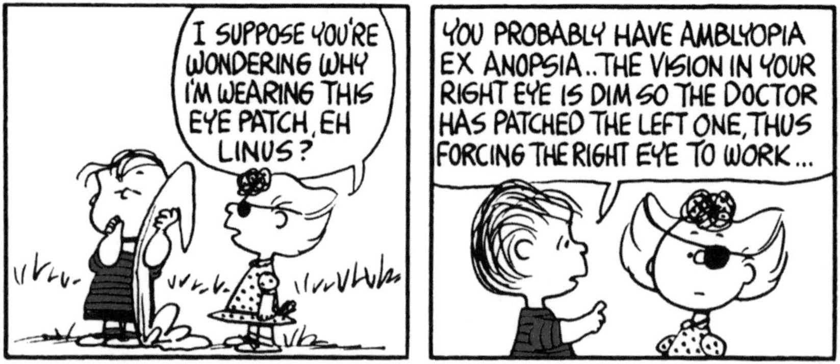
I SUPPOSE YOU'RE WONDERING WHY I'M WEARING THIS EYE PATCH, EH LINUS?
YOU PROBABLY HAVE AMBLYOPIA EX ANOPSIA..THE VISION IN YOUR RIGHT EYE IS DIM SO THE DOCTOR HAS PATCHED THE LEFT ONE, THUS FORCING THE RIGHT EYE TO WORK...

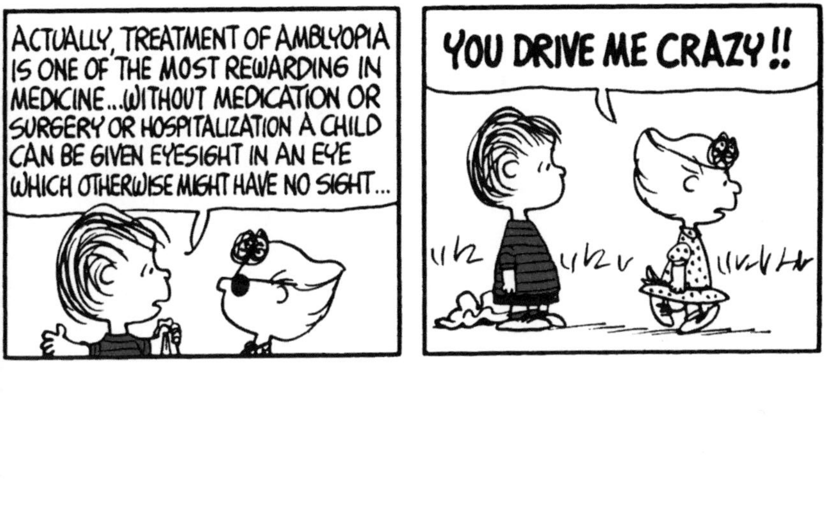
ACTUALLY, TREATMENT OF AMBLYOPIA IS ONE OF THE MOST REWARDING IN MEDICINE...WITHOUT MEDICATION OR SURGERY OR HOSPITALIZATION A CHILD CAN BE GIVEN EYESIGHT IN AN EYE WHICH OTHERWISE MIGHT HAVE NO SIGHT...
YOU DRIVE ME CRAZY!!

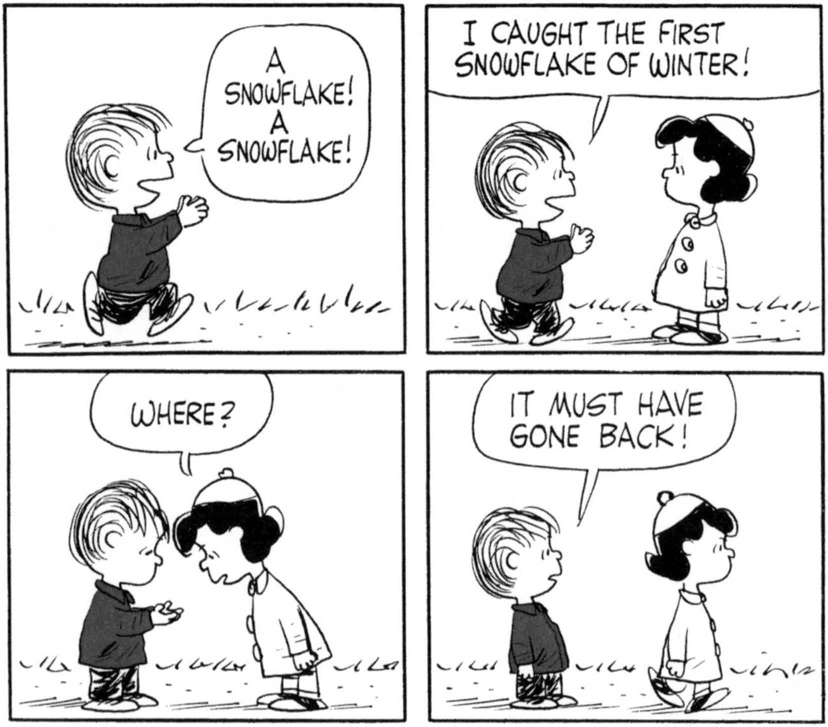
A SNOWFLAKE! A SNOWFLAKE!
I CAUGHT THE FIRST SNOWFLAKE OF WINTER!
WHERE?
IT MUST HAVE GONE BACK!

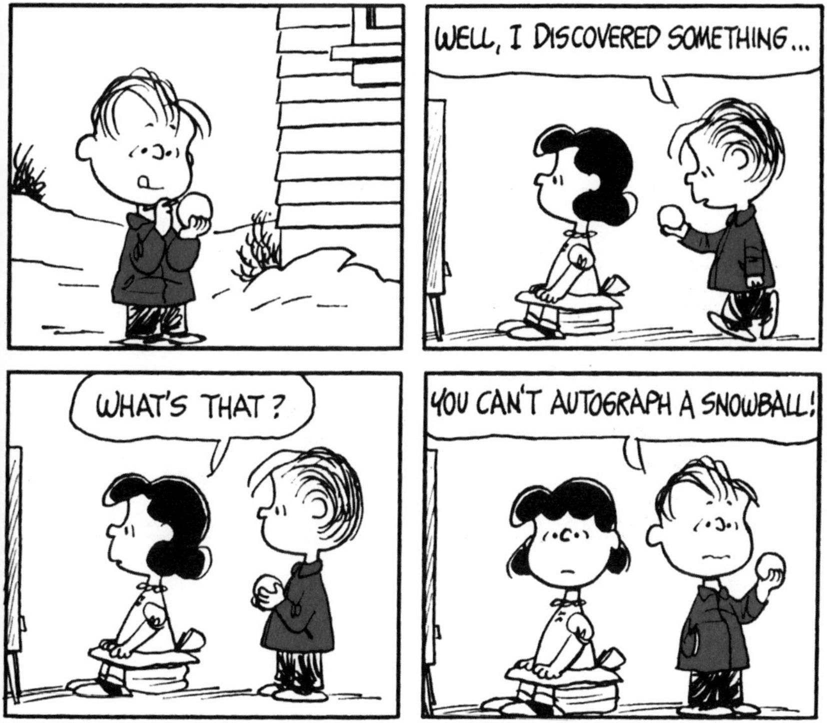
WELL, I DISCOVERED SOMETHING...
WHAT'S THAT?
YOU CAN'T AUTOGRAPH A SNOWBALL!

PEOPLE ARE BEGINNING TO SAY NASTY THINGS ABOUT ME
I'M SORRY, BLANKET... I'M GOING TO HAVE TO LEAVE YOU HERE BY THE SIDE OF THE ROAD!

IT WAS WHIMPERING!

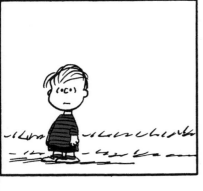

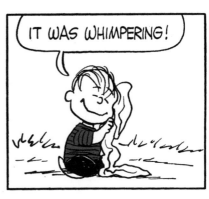

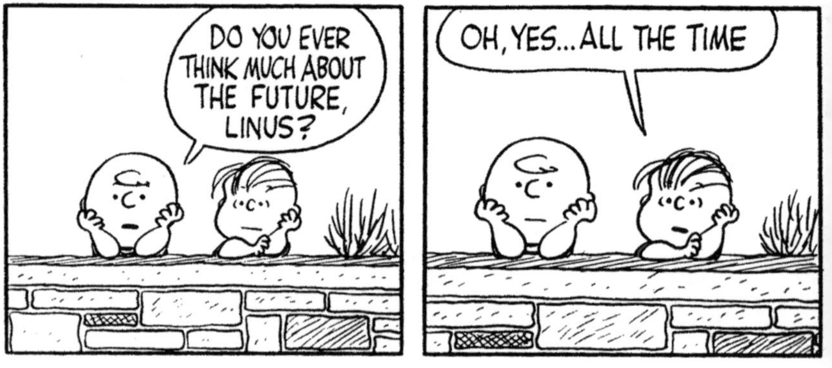
DO YOU EVER THINK MUCH ABOUT THE FUTURE, LINUS?
OH, YES...ALL THE TIME

WHAT DO YOU THINK YOU'D LIKE TO BE WHEN YOU GROW UP?
OUTRAGEOUSLY HAPPY!

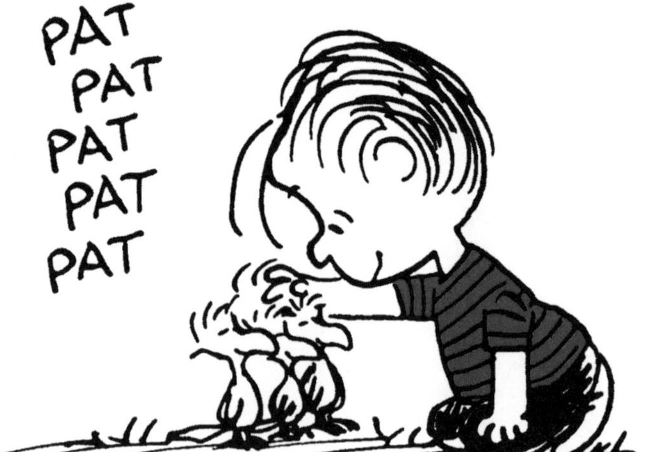
PAT
PAT
PAT
PAT
PAT